The Stroke of
Favor:
The Call

"A look at the calling, purpose, and favor of God on your life."

By
Michael D. Ward

Copyright © 2014 by Rev. Michael D. Ward

The Stroke of Favor: The Call
"A look at the calling, purpose, and favor of God on your life."
by Rev. Michael D. Ward

Printed in the United States of America

ISBN 9781498400367

All rights reserved solely by the author. The author guarantees all contents are original and do not infringe upon the legal rights of any other person or work. No part of this book may be reproduced in any form without the permission of the author. The views expressed in this book are not necessarily those of the publisher.

Scripture quotations taken from the New King James Version (NKJV). Copyright © 1979, 1980, 1982 by Thomas Nelson, Inc. Used by permission. All rights reserved.

Scripture quotations taken from the New American Standard Bible (NASB). Copyright © 1960, 1962, 1963, 1968, 1971, 1972, 1973, 1975, 1977, 1995 by The Lockman Foundation. Used by permission. All rights reserved.

Scripture quotations taken from the New International Version (NIV). Copyright © 1973, 1978, 1984, 2011 by Biblica, Inc.™. Used by permission. All rights reserved.

Scripture quotations marked HCSB are from the Holman Christian Standard Bible®. HCSB®. Copyright ©1999, 2000, 2002, 2003 by Holman Bible Publishers. Used by permission. Holman Christian Standard Bible®, Holman CSB®, and HCSB® are federally registered trademarks of Holman Bible Publishers

www.xulonpress.com

TABLE OF CONTENTS

Foreword vii

Introduction ix

Chapter 1: The Total Call 11

Chapter 2: No Regrets 21

Chapter 3: The Making of a Man/Woman of God:
             The Call of Moses 29

Chapter 4: The Unmatchable Offering: The Call of Samuel . . . 37

Chapter 5: The Long Way to Purpose: The Call of Jonah 43

Chapter 6: The Ultimate Call: The Call of Jeremiah 51

Chapter 7: The Importance of Mentorship in your Calling:
             The Calling of Elisha 57

Chapter 8: Events From the Vision 63

Chapter 9:   Personal Time Ministry 69

Chapter 10: Where From Here 73

Chapter 11: God's Favor in the call 77

Foreword

"We are confident, I say, and willing rather to be absent from the body, and to be present with the Lord." (2 Corinthians 5:8)

As I sit in my living room enjoying the company of my brother who was written off by medical prognosis, declared incapable of recovery by doctors, doubted by nurses, deemed questionable by some family and friends, I am in total awe of the Power of God!! I want to shout to the nations "Hallelujah" at the top of my lungs, for this truly is The Lord's doing, and it is marvelous in my eyes!

I glance over at his wife as she recounts the seconds, minutes, hours, days, weeks, and months that led up to this moment in our living room. As she gives my wife and me a glimpse into her moment of concern during the recovery process, she shares a moment that made her heart melt at one of the facilities where my brother was in therapy. He was asked, "What day and month is it?" His response, based on what his wife had shared, was the actual date he had the stroke. His wife shared that in this moment fear gripped her, and she was overwhelmed with concern that her husband might not be the same ever again.

Well, she was right, but not as some may believe. In that moment, God spoke a word that would bring peace, clarity, and understanding to what my brother's time asleep (or in a coma some say) was really all about: He was absent from his body, but he was present with The Lord!

God said that He is not bound or constrained by time, so it is only logical that my brother's lack of knowledge of the progression of time was demonstrated when asked the date. God does not exist in time as we do, but He does step into time and assist us in our now. God, Himself, desired an audience with my brother, to show him all the things that He had in store for his life and to reaffirm the call and favor that He had placed on his life before he was in his mother's womb.

Prepare yourself for a journey, buckle up for an adventure, and prepare your heart to experience the passion of a man whom The Lord chose to give an opportunity to step out of time and into the eternal presence of The Almighty God! Lord, let us become more aware of Your Presence.

— Rev James Bridgewater

Introduction

"Desire spiritual gifts, especially to prophesy."
(1 Corinthians 14:1, NKJV)

One of the reasons people miss out on the call of God is they have a misunderstanding of exactly what it is He's calling them to do. The calling of God is multifaceted, calling for a great variety of options geared specifically for each Christian involved. The scary thing about the calling is knowing it has the ability to change during the seasons of our lives. Many people think the calling only involves preaching. Because they might be terrified of public speaking, they are quick to say no. We have to realize that a versatile God who demonstrated His preference in an event like creation also wants His children serving Him in a plurality of roles. He's not solely calling people to preach. He's also calling evangelists, missionaries, artists, musicians, writers, poets, and teachers to minister, just to name a few.

The calling of a prophet would definitely have to have God's imprint all over it. The specialty of such a role is very challenging. Not only will people doubt you were sent to them, but you may doubt yourself. This is a common feeling when handling the calling of God, due to the amount of time previously spent building self-reliance to now having it stripped away by God to serve Him (John 3:30, NKJV).

So, in this book, we will discuss various prophets in the Bible as we examine the many ways God calls man to serve Him with different mandates on their lives.

At the end of this book, you will find opportunities to participate with personal questions and perform certain exercises. The study guide is designed from the Holy Spirit to assist your decision making in regards to God's calling. Everyday people choose to pass God's desire because they overlook His calling. Remember that your life is no longer yours. Giving of yourself is for Him because He is the giver of life and every good gift is from above (James 1:17, NKJV). I hope that you enjoy reading and learning from this book and view it as one of His gifts.

Chapter 1

THE TOTAL CALL

> If it is true you look favorably on me, let me know your ways so I may understand you more fully and continue to enjoy your favor. (Exodus 33:13, NKJV)

Have you ever wondered what your purpose is? Why were you born? Why are you here? Are you doing the right things with your life? Have you, or are you battling with making a decision to accept God's call? If you responded yes to any of these questions, or you are not sure, then this is a good book for you.

Before we get started, there is a more important reason as to know why a person would feel empty or meaningless in the face of these questions: The reason may be you are missing a relationship with Jesus Christ, and that you might need to personally invite Him into your heart. Ensure that you have a personal relationship with the giver of purpose: Jesus Christ; not only does He give you a purpose, but He gives you His life.

Yes, a relationship with Him; a relationship is between two parties that know, care, love, and are genuinely concerned about each other's well-being more than their own. Galatians 2:20 says that we have been crucified with Christ, it is no longer I who lives but Christ who lives in me; and the life which I now live is in the flesh in the son of God, who loved me and gave Himself for me." A prime example of a relationship would be Jonathan and David in the book of 1 Samuel. Jesus accomplished His purpose for coming to the earth, and he is indeed the one worthy to have a relationship with. It is for this reason that we live, move, and have our being through Him. If you have not accepted Jesus Christ, I invite you to set this book down at this moment and make Jesus Christ your Lord and Savior in your heart through praying for His presence to be within you. When we exist without purpose, our life makes no sense and comes to a turning point or dead end.

When life almost came to a screeching stop for me in 2013, my story was the exact opposite. On the top of my life, I was living out my calling in bliss on a daily basis with a great wife, kids, and working as a chaplain at the County jail. Nevertheless, on Tuesday, June 25, 2013, I found myself unconscious and in a coma for five days in the Neurological Intensive Care Unit. It turns out that I suffered from a very severe hemorrhagic stroke on both sides of my brain.

The medical experts could not understand how anyone could survive from this type of brain trauma, as statistics show that only two out of seven people survive from this type of stroke. The report showed that I would not survive through the night or the next day, and after that they said I would live but I would be lucky to be a vegetable. We found out on an MRI three months later that the pond of the brain stem area was completely empty, whereas at the time of the stroke three months earlier it was full of blood. A real twenty-first-century documental and proven miracle, as the healing power of God's hands caused the pond of the brain stem to become like new and undamaged.

In reflection upon my call, I explored to see if any aspects of my calling had disobedience in them. I did not find any. What was revealed to me was that, although I didn't have any disobedience or sin in my calling, it was time to move to a higher arena. Outside of the hand of God, there were also four special inmates in my program that acted as my heroes during this occurrence. When I collapsed and my office called 911, my colleagues were instructed to have the patient (me) downstairs to the clinic for inmates, and the ambulance would pick me up. When the four inmates (Ronnie, Quincy, Michael, and Marcus) could not get me from the sixth floor to the first floor because the elevators were down, they carried me down six flights of stairs. While at the jail's clinic, a doctor gave me a shot to the neck to help improve recovery in case I was having a stroke. The Lord's hand was even in this, as it turns out that I went to church with him and his family twenty years ago. Romans 8:28 resounded as truth in this instance "All things work together for good to those who love God and to those who are called according to His purpose." This entire turn of events demonstrates God's favor towards me, in that my Neuroscience surgeon said the doctor's shot at the jail was a blood thinner, and I should have bled to death since I was having a hemorrhagic stroke. It was His touch that superseded man's law.

On the day of my stroke, I went to a hole-in-the-wall Mexican restaurant and ate an enchilada dinner that soared my blood pressure to 243/143. In addition, my temperature grew to 110 degree, and the fever lasted for a week. The chances for survival looked slim. But God had other intentions, as the righteous of God was set aside for more work. Psalm 34:19 says it best, "many are the afflictions of the righteous, but God delivers us out of them all." Yes, He does. No matter what you are facing.

A second kind of stroke, known as a schematic stroke, has a higher level of survivability but can also be very fatal. This is a highly overlooked topic in our culture. As a matter of fact, Stroke Prevention Month is during the month of May, but my stroke happened in June. I never heard one commercial on either TV or radio, not a flyer, a poster, or a distributed sticker about stroke prevention. There was not any warning for me to watch out for a stroke. There is no one to blame but myself. But no matter what you're facing or what your report is, remember you're already victorious in Christ.

There's not anything new the enemy can throw your way. The scripture reminds us that we are mindful and equipped to stand up to the schemes of the devil (Ephesians 6:11). A scheme requires some planning or equipping. With God's preparation, we are ready. Through faith, as I have told my thousands of inmates that I minister to, "God is not punishing us, He is preparing us." In calling you, what is He preparing you for?

In my call, I have had eighteen years of experience and have not done many things outside of the tradition of a minister: preaching in a church, going on short term mission trips, performing weddings, baptisms, and conducting the Lord's Supper.

The thing to understand about purpose is that there are various levels for our purpose in life, depending on our state of maturity. It is very possible to have one purpose at twenty years old and a different one at forty years old. The main thing that is your responsibility is obedience.

Was there a moment in your life that you felt you missed the mark? You have yet to discover the reason you were born, or if that time is still to come. If it has not, were you supposed to be still and be ready for God's timing? There is a moment in time that defines each person's life. In this book, we will uncover various aspects to help us all discover if we have experienced that moment in time.

This book will have you prepared for that moment. There is a common misconception that everyone does not have a moment, but I beg to differ. We are all created for a purpose, a role, or an assignment that we must complete in this lifetime. Be encouraged if you think you already missed your moment. Remind yourself that our God is a God that continues to give us multiple chances. Each day holds new opportunities and chances in God. (Lamentations 3:17) I'm confident that if I had not survived that stroke my purpose would have still been fulfilled, because each purpose is succeeded by the next one that we do not know about in the future.

So let's explore deeper into this reading, and enjoy it as you are challenged to go deeper in your walk with God and fulfill your purpose. We will also discuss visions and dreams according what I've discovered based on personal experiences and biblical facts (Joel 2:28). Then we will look at biblical characters as well as others since then that have undergone some amazing life transformations as a result of the decision to submit to God. So sit back and examine, enjoy, and be challenged to review your own life for revelation and insight.

There are three aspects of the total call: obedience, competence, and humility. Many people see these criteria and wonder why I did not included knowledge or confidence. If you think about it, you will realize those are both self-reliant attributes. Obedience is often realized by the called when a decision to forsake sin in their lives and completely commit to God through fear of Him is made. The trait of competence is when a person has truly trusted in God for the success of their accomplishments. The final ingredient of the godly call would be humility. James 1:9 says that "humble people should feel important because of their high position."

For example, an athlete that is in God has only made it to the National Football League by God's blessings of grace, mercy, kindness, love, peace, many other intangible spiritual gifts, and of course, favor. He could have been in the same category as millions of others who were skilled enough but did not make it.

This is not about status but rather an internal spiritual condition as we grow in the spirit by God. We see that the word shares that God opposes the proud but gives grace to the humble. Grace is such a mystery in regards to God's gifts and His mercy. He spares us when we should be removed and keeps us for His purpose.

As we look deeper into these three aspects of the total call, obedience is first and should be an aspect that every Christian possesses as they move toward maturation. Competence is demonstrated when the believer has the ability to research the Scriptures, discern the voice of God, and be committed to following God's vision. While humility is a choice mandated by God so that the believer will not take any credit for himself but gives God the glory and can be trusted.

Throughout this book, we will discuss various personal instances where I was forced to write this book by the Lord. I hope this will be a useful tool for you as you discuss with your loved ones if your calling will require anything special, challenging, or committing.

Many feel their past may disqualify them from a calling, but everyone is eligible for the calling of God. We do not have the right to neglect the call of God; remember, it is His doing and calling for each of us. He created us; we did not create ourselves. Psalm 139:13 states, "For you created my inmost being; you knit me together in my mother's womb." This shows His predominance and ownership over everything, including you, the earth, our possessions, and the future. Now that we have discussed the fact that God has ownership over everything, we can begin to explore the call, and hopefully you will discover additional details of your purpose.

2 Peter 1:10 encourages us to be sure of our calling and election so that we will not stumble into sin. So, as you can see, your calling and election play a big role in your Christian walk.

Since we all have a role in the body of Christ, we all must be committed to do our part with excellence built on top of our faith (2 Peter 1:5). Excellence is not always practiced at all levels of ministries or in handling the calling. In this book, you will discover some traits to help identify what you are dealing with. The made up mind regarding the calling will always strive to seek and experience God in a spiritual manner. Just because you are having success doesn't mean that you are not going to experience any difficulty. Scripture teaches us how to handle this adversity and understanding, because the race is not given to the swift or the fastest but to the one who endures (Eccl 9:11, NKJV).

Chapter 1 Review

A TIME OF REFLECTION

1. What have you felt was your life's purpose up to this point?

2. How would you have defined "total call" prior to this chapter?

3. Besides saving the chaplain's life, what effect in their spiritual lives do you think carrying him down six flight of stairs might have had on the four inmates?

4. What are the two types of strokes? Describe them please.

5. Why might you think everyone is eligible for the call?

Chapter 2

NO REGRETS

"For the gifts and calling of God are without repentance." (Romans 11:29, NLT)

We have repented of our sins, or least prayed to consider it, but how would one attempt to repent of his calling? As soon as one accepts God's calling and recognizes what God's gifts are, he should display a spirit of gratefulness rather than repentance. If one has moral failures walking in God's calling, he should repent not because of his calling but his sin.

God's calling is specific with individuals. You can choose it maturely or immaturely, responsibly or irresponsibly, with or without a sense of urgency. Regardless, one must be prepared to face whatever consequences lie within.

In this life, we try to figure out why things happen to people. Man wonders about things such as what the historian Dietrich Bonhoeffer thought about when he wrote, "Why do bad things happen to good people?" They figure that the good person must have had some sin issue in his life. But, from personal perspective, that is not always the case. My stroke was not based on obedience or disobedience, but it was preparation for a higher calling. That was also the case with the man born blind in John 9. They asked the question, "Did this man sin or his parents?" Jesus responded that, "Neither sinned, it was that the work of the Father that may be glorified."

The first day I was at the hospital, as I said before, the medical staff told my boss, Mike Barber, and my wife, Danielle, that I would not make it through the night. When I did make it, they said that I would be a vegetable for life. So Mike told them to get out of the way with their decision and let God take over. My, did He ever! His favor was toward me in a special way. I must continue to walk with Him in all the days of my life.

My wife was operating with supernatural faith, although everyone thought that she was in denial. She trusted God big, and He was her rewarder of faith (Hebrews 11:6). I was released from the second hospital with full memory function and about ninety percent of my physical body functioning. Once again, this stroke was so serious that many called my recovery and healing a miracle.

As I recall the visions (to be discussed later) that I experienced in the coma, it truly was a miracle. The coma was an act of God, as he allowed me to experience some healing during this time. While in the coma for five days, I experienced God in a very unique ways. First of all, He told me it was not my time to come to Heaven because He already had me. Now note, I am not making a claim that I ever saw God, because no man can do that and live. His voice, though, was very evident, and I am alive!

Many people in our society undergo a health crisis, but is it not until later they realize the significance that it plays in their calling in life. Romans 8:28 states that all things work together for the good of those who love God and are called according to His purpose. You see, that is precisely the point, we are all called by God. We want things to work out our way in life, to experience His goodness in life. It is our God who enhanced us in this life to be followed for a lifetime by goodness and mercy throughout our life. Matthew 6:33 declares for us to seek the kingdom of God and His righteousness and all things will be added to you.

It was revealed to me that we will often operate in our calling on cruise control. Being on cruise control in the faith is the reason that many Christians miss out on their destination. What would have happened had Abraham stopped sojourning after rescuing Lot? Or what would have happened if King Hezekiah had given up after discovering he was sick? Both instances show us to be persistent and prayerful as a commitment to our faith. How did adversity occur if I was called, had His favor, and was living in obedience? I was shown that we will often operate in our calling on cruise control, or ordinary living within it, when we are not ready to accept a new challenge of obedience from God. It is as if that is not necessary daily, it is only used in crucial times of adversity. During these various times, the body of Christ must "walk by faith and not by sight" (2 Corinthians 5:7). Seeing the outcome before performing the action is crucial in appreciating the realization to aid in future belief and remain faithful.

The true confession for believers everywhere is often that we are not ready to accept a new challenge of obedience from God. In 2 Timothy 2:2, He calls for us to entrust these things to faithful men. What are "these things?" The writer was referencing a call for the men of the church to be strong in their commitment to the Lord and His teachings. It is ironic that this problem existed in both the early church as well as in today's church, and is still a main concern as we are assisting those exploring the call of God on their life. We would live in a perfect world if men rose up and accepted their call, operated in obedience, and turned their back from sin.

The best way to understand the role of men in ministry, as well as of mankind, is to explore the various examples that we have seen in the Holy Bible. After having witnessed God complete many wonders and miracles in my lifetime, I wonder if my stroke was my moment in time. The answer is yes, it was one of them.

After awakening from the stroke, I reflected back over my life and realized a mixture of holy as well as unholy activity. Although I accepted my call into ministry on November 8, 1999, I still had a lot of unfinished worldly living. My calling shows that God can call and use anyone.

At the time of my calling, God found me in a nightclub with two alcoholic beverages in my hands; and He immediately put me to work for his glory. He had me quit a $100,000 a year job, drop the two drinks and the two girls that I was dancing with in the club, and go to work in full-time ministry before placing me on the mission field. I thought that was what my life was to be, but there was another chapter coming later that I'm discovering.

Experiencing the stroke was a lot like discovering Jesus Christ as your Lord and Savior. First of all, whenever you go through a time of medical care in the hospital, as I did, I compare it to the infant stages of being a Christian. After the infancy stage, you endure stages of growth and healing where rehabilitation may have to take place, like our Christian walks. When you're in the hospital stage, you're receiving constant care and nurture and in Christian life it should be the same after you are born again. But many people feel we have to do it alone, which leads to early and often failures in our Christian lives.

We were not meant to do it alone because we are a collective unit as the body of Christ. We have to call on others to make this journey of the Christian walk victorious, successful, and prosperous. So when we are deciding what to do with this call, we have to solicit the advice from the body of Christ after spending exclusive time with God.

The total call is composed of the divine call, which is a total of life's experiences and a pathway of spiritual experiences. As discovered in personal debates, the mainstream school of theological thought feels that using life experiences are invalid in seeing God's hand over your life during your calling experience. Many in the theological community feel that your life feelings do not play a role in experiences. They feel your salvific experience should not include life experiences. This makes sense because your salvation should focus on the gospel of Christ and be built up on discipleship your Christian life. The life experience segment is important from the standpoint of personalizing the Gospel where men and women can obtain a personal relationship with Jesus Christ. This relationship is mandatory and the first step before accepting a call to ministry before God.

Is Jesus truly in charge of your life? Many people say yes, but He is really not. He is called upon when there is trouble, but He wants to do so much more. He wants to give approval on the small decisions as well as the major ones, so He can get the glory. We have to arrive at the choice to make our lives pleasurable to Him. Remember that God is a spirit, and those who worship Him, worship Him in spirit and truth (John 4:24). That means all we do, we do for Him.

Chapter 2 Review

A Time of Reflection

1. What was miraculous about the whole health crisis in correlation to the call?

2. What are the "these things" in your life as mentioned in 2 Timothy 2:2?

3. What has been the defining moment of time of your life?

4. What should happen immediately after a person is born again?

5. Name a way that Christ is in charge of your life.

Chapter 3

THE MAKING OF A MAN/ WOMAN OF GOD: THE CALL OF MOSES

"Let every man abide in the same calling wherein he was called was called." (1 Corinthians 7:20, KJV)

Exactly what calling of God are you in? Are you viewing your calling as talent instead of God's instrument at work for Him? Look at Moses in Exodus 4:20, where his shepherd's staff is referred to as the staff of God. Everything we have belongs to Him, and He knows where you are in life, what your condition is, and what you can do.

Let's compare the call of Moses to the one in our lives. First of all, we understand that Moses is an enshrined figure in both Christian and Jewish culture. Why? What did he have to do in order to be this?

Is it due to him being a central figure as a hero of the faith in both the Pentateuch and the Holy Bible? Or was it his calling event? Many have differing opinions, but they do agree that they feel a sense of Moses within themselves and admire his faithfulness, which is a key feature to the call.

Just as all of us, Moses operated and lived with the favor of God. There was not one friend necessary for him to bounce things off of. He demonstrated this through his faith, as he never questioned God but overcame weaknesses of his own strength and abilities. He shows us this in his relationship with God. If you think about it, no one would have believed you if you started talking about a burning bush that would not stop burning, or about the voice of God within that bush, or about being on holy ground in a pasture. The feeling that Moses exclaimed when he saw that the bush was not being consumed while burning was "amazing." This is what we are to expect to feel at the acceptance of God's calling. Life is now supposed to become amazing. Not to say that every day is to going to be great or rewarding, but your perspective will be enhanced. The mind of Christ will grow stronger due to God's guidance and presence.

Just as those who have experienced denial towards God, we see that Moses does as well. Internally he had to be thinking about his upbringing, the murderer, living in the Egyptian culture, being single, his dead end job as a shepherd, etc. As in all accounts of the call of God, He calls his name to get his attention, as if Goes does not know him. Through the calling of his name, Moses should have known that the facts about his whole life were known. But still he was being called. God knows us and wants us to succeed in our calling. He always calls us by name, just as any friend would do.

Callings are not a wait and see decision; they are a yes or no decision. It is never to say that God will never come back to you if you say no. Be advised, however, that it is not wise to tell a loving God that you are not ready to work for Him. In fact, that's the perfect time to say yes when you want to say no, so that your decision is on Him and not yourself.

As we continue this exploration, we find Moses operating in his role as the shepherd. Often times, we find ourselves operating in a vocational field occurring within context of our calling. For example, a farmer that hosts a weekly Bible study with the local farmhands should not find it surprising to be called the city's Pastor in the small local church. His Bible study was a preview of what he was willing to be in God. He is still a farmer who now views the growth of spiritual lives as more important than taking care of animals and plants.

That is the way it is in all of our lives. Whatever we have been in the natural life, God will use that for His glory and for His purpose. If you were a quarterback in football, then your skills and gifting of leadership are on you and will most likely be used by God in your life if you allow Him to. Or perhaps you were the center on the volleyball team that prepared you for leadership, whereas now your role is as a corporate professional leading the way, which can further get you ready to receive your calling. There is a reason as to why we have been where weeping was necessary, and why we made it through for a purpose and time that we know nothing about. Jeremiah 33:3 shows a picture of an imprisoned Jeremiah, and the Lord says to call upon Him and He will show us great and wonderful things which we know nothing about. We must simply trust Him, because we do not know what's around the curve, but He does. In a sense, He is our map or navigation system, and we must depend upon Him for our every move for the duration of our lives.

There is no turning the car off and stopping and falling away. Moses did just that. One moment he was resting at a well in Midian when the highlight of his life was beginning, and the next he was defending some girls that were being chased by some shepherds, who were simply hired hands. The shepherds were manning a position, a job, not a calling, but after Moses rose up and defended the girls, he took over their roles. God is constantly calling and equipping us, and we must be faithful in ministering before Him.

We must operate in our callings before Him and not try to impress people. In our calling, it doesn't matter whether you're a pastor, schoolteacher, missionary, committed professional, or a community activist, you still have a need to defend those to whom you minister. Defending is not always physical, but it may be spiritual, verbal, or supporting a cause or position.

However, we discover through Moses that the total call is composed of the divine call to reflect upon your life experiences, to witness and identify His grace over your life, and finally to realize how you previously handled the issue and repent to do better in the future.

As we look at Moses' past and the influence it had on his calling, it might seem strange that he took out his anguish of being in the Egyptian population against of all things, an Egyptian. Was he defending the race he turned away from by guilt, or was he responding to peer pressure to prove that indeed he was one of the Egyptians? Not only the authorities viewed Moses as a murderer, but he did as well. Imagine, had he disqualified himself, he wouldn't have gone on to defend the children of Israel. Examine yourself briefly to make sure you have reconciled your past before continuing forth in the journey of your calling.

As you accept your calling, are you prepared to take some initiative in ministry? If someone calls with a special problem dealing with ministry, what do you do? Well the answer to that is first pray, then let those parties know that you have to handle it in the morning. This is for preservation of self so that we know that God is in control and not we ourselves.

God was not in control of Moses' situation until He got his attention. Moses was reactive. It was not until Moses rested by the well in Midian forty years later that God was in control. When we get tired of being in our own effort, it is only then that we have a tendency to surrender to God. Let's try giving our best to Him upfront.

Moses was in the right place at the right time when he was at the well. That experience led him toward his calling. It is pretty amazing that Moses was born for this event of life and had made some life delaying events. In your calling, be open to God using an enemy at your occupation to launch you in your calling, just as Moses dealt with curiosity of the things of God. Like Moses' view of the burning bush, we must take a similar stance as God shows Himself in an unusual way that we are not accustomed to. Our not knowing about spiritual things in the early stages of our life creates a curiosity into the unknown. The bush was a fire that was not being consumed by the fire. This fire represents the presence of God. God's nature is not one of destruction but is to nourish, equip, fulfill, provide for, heal, and forgive. He allowed Moses to accept those attributes that are necessary in the beginning stages to receive His call.

The making of the man of God reveals God as the Master. It can make us useful what man deemed as useless (Philemon 1:11). In the calling, he takes our imperfections and combines them with His perfection.

We turn our life of imperfections over to Him. He allows the Holy Spirit to join in with His perfection and make a success out of you. He wants to call you: if you are blind, He wants to call you; if you can't talk, He wants to call you; if you have a learning problem, He wants to call you; anything qualifies you.

As long as there is breath in your body, He can use you. Are you available? That's often a question that is posed to anyone volunteering a service. It's a heart commitment. The call has to be from the heart. Moses had curiosities and love for his biological people: the children of Israel. He was more likely feeling worthless and unfulfilled after growing up in Egyptian culture and existing as one of them. His calling is a story of redemption. He withstood the various tests of God to prove something he wanted. Since he had waited forty years already, God knew He had just the right man to deal with Pharaoh's stubbornness. What was really attractive was Moses' obedience, which is a 100% necessary when accepting the call of God.

Chapter 3 Review

A TIME OF REFLECTION

1. How does not burning out in the burning bush relate to your life with God?

2. Please describe what a "hired hand" looks like in today's church?

3. Why was Moses even up at Mt. Sinai? Were you at an unpredictable place during your call?

4. What was the motive behind Moses killing the Egyptian? Do you have any deep seated emotional issues that you must confront?

5. What are some key personality issues you've prayed for God to cover while operating in His calling?

Chapter 4

THE UNMATCHABLE OFFERING: THE CALL OF SAMUEL

"I call you therefore, I the prisoner of the Master, all you to walk in a matter worthy of the calling which you have been called." (Ephesians 4:1, NKJV)

Samuel was called by the Lord three times before finally replying, "Here I am Lord." (1 Samuel 3:4). That must be our response. A common thing we see in people called by God is that He uses our first names to address the attention of men and women. Why is that? A safe assumption is, since He knew you before the foundation of the world, He already has familiarity with you on a first name basis. He has already written your name down in the Lamb's book of life (Revelation 13:8) because it was from there that we learned the Lord's instructions for you.

In verse 1 of chapter 3 in the book of 1 Samuel, we see that as a boy Samuel was already in service under Eli's supervision. He fulfills the aspect of immediately submitting to authority as we all must do as part of meeting the satisfaction of acquiring the call of God. As the called of God, we must continue to manage our household as a first priority. The home is one of numerous references in scripture that show a visible identifier to the spiritual health of the minister. Eli failed miserably in this area with his two sons, Hophni and Phineas. By judging from the outcome of their character as described in Scripture, Eli must have missed too many games as well as more developmental activities; many forsake similar events in the name of ministry. Eli accepted his calling as a prophet, but missed his calling into fatherhood. He was led by compassion but lacked correction. Many in ministry, the corporate world, or other involvements make the wrong decision in the area of family life. Your child will only be a child once, so seize the moment. God will never have you choose something over your family.

At this stage of life, Eli was having regrets about the way he raised his boys. They were defiling the altar and women, and were only concerned about personal gain. This is a trait many ministers and lay members have adopted based on career failures, life interruptions due to ministry, or for ministerial games to keep up with their peers.

The second fulfillment of the call is the importance of advisement mentorship. When Samuel didn't know what was happening, he went over to Eli, thinking that Eli was calling him. So Eli told him to lie back down and wait to give his response. One thing that both Samuel and Eli are credited with is a dependency of God to speak again, and this plays a huge role in the calling. Hearing and discerning the will of God and not man is focal in the call. Samuel was donated to the temple at a time when The Lord was not there. His mother, Hannah, remained faithful in spite of her current circumstances. She knew that although God was not there He was to be worshipped in Shiloh, and without the donation of her son, the current conditions would not change.

Eli, on other hand, had two grown sons that were serving as crooked priests, not giving honor to their father. As a result, the failure to discipline them cost Eli his life on the same day as his sons. The call has implications that fall on others, such as missed chances at salvation, other divine appointments, and even death with unfulfilled purpose (1 Samuel 4:18). As shown in 1 Samuel 3:7, it points out very importantly that Samuel did not yet know The Lord. Based on this scripture, we see that God calls and uses anyone He desires. If the unsaved are called, there is a major plan at work. Without the presence of God at Shiloh during Samuel's day, it is understandable how someone would not be called. The odds of Samuel being born when his mother was barren were rare, but they actually were turned to his parent's favor because of their contact with a prophet.

Under Samuel's prophetic leadership, we see him as the prophet chosen by God to select the man after God's own heart, David.

Examine yourself and ask if Eli captured his life's purpose in the way he handled Samuel or his two sons?

Samuel was active in service since the beginning of kingship in Israel. He saw the example of a good king who eventually had to be removed because of disobedience to God's instructions (Saul). This led to Saul's anointing being taken away by God, as well as his authority as king. This is a prime example of what called men and women of God face when denying or mishandling the call of God. Although King Saul sinned against God, Samuel did not remove him; but God did through his death. Samuel, as well as King David, who was Saul's replacement, showed the importance of how your service before appointment would equal up to your calling. Before his election as king of Israel, David served as shepherd over sheep. Both events mirrored Christ in understanding that man came to serve and not to be served. Are you serving from the pureness of your heart, or are you seeking a selfish motive?

Chapter 4 Review

A TIME OF REFLECTION

1. Name how and to whom you have submitted to authority?

2. Where did Eli go wrong with parenting his boys?

3. What was he doing wrong with his sons that ministers should never do?

4. Is it possible for an unsaved person to be called in today's world? Explain.

5. Please describe the advisement mentorship relationship in your life.

Chapter 5

THE LONG WAY TO PURPOSE: THE CALL OF JONAH

> When Isaac planted that year, he harvested a hundred times more than he planted, God blessed him. (Genesis 26:12 NLT)

As a called believer of God, it goes without saying that the principle of extraordinary returns occurs when you invest with God. Jonah's fear and prejudices caused him to not focus on the rate of return, but to look at his own personal commitment. It was not the return he pictured, so he evacuated. Jonah was selected by God to go down and pronounce judgment to the people in Nineveh as his calling. As we examine how Jonah approached his calling, it is safe to say that, due to lack of being knowledgeable and experienced in this area of their Christian walk, the majority of men and women handle the calling just as Jonah did. He ran from God in a blatant and intentional manner. Unlike many in our culture, Jonah had inaccurate information about what it meant to be called. The good thing is that he had the chance to ask questions and offer excuses directly to God after he was approached. There are some people that refuse to research the call, but instead make their own decision without knowing the truth.

If Jonah had known the truth before going through his trial, the truth would have set him free long before he was disciplined by God. His fear and rebellion led to capturing himself. Yes, things such as lies, stealing, killing, or any other cowardly sin will lead us into self- incarceration.

In our decisions in life, we often have to learn from previous mistakes before being set free. Freedom has to be the aim for all Christians. Imagine if you had freedom over your family, your finances, all your relations, and your future. It would make a difference, right? Once a person has received salvation, they should have obtained their freedom, but that is not the always the case. In maturation, we learn that where the spirit of The Lord is there is freedom (2 Corinthians 3:17). So, make the decision that affects your life for now and in eternity.

Imagine, running from God to a country known for sin and it's prosperous trade commerce, and where it was known that His presence was not there. As a result of all of Jonah's escape tactics, God used His control of the weather to control Jonah's circumstances regarding his calling. You may have denied or avoided His calling twelve years ago, but you experienced some extreme situations that only God could have brought you through. He may have kept you to deliver a tough message because you were born for it. Operating in your calling is the best life for you. So, the decision is not if I want to receive His calling, but rather do I want to live the best possible life that He has for me?

As Esther became the queen of Israel, Her uncle Mordecai declared unto her, "You were born for a time such as this." Jonah was suffering from fear and prejudice. Those were the causes of his disobedience. 2 Timothy 1:7 says, "God did not give us the spirit of fear but of love, power, and a sound mind." This scripture holds true as we face a decision about His calling. When fear is present, we fail to see God›s love, use His power, or utilize the soundness of our minds.

As we think about the calling, a sound mind would have you consider the original prophet, Abraham. He was commanded to sacrifice his only and long awaited son, Isaac. In your calling, have you been asked to do the uncertain? Anytime faith is necessary, there will always be a more noticeable presence of uncertainty that the enemy has placed to turn one away.

We must know that God can use any environment you are in to reach those around you. We see that while Jonah was running, and on the boat to Tarsus, the captain of his ship came to Jonah and asked him to pray to God.

In dealing with his calling, Jonah became very angry in Jonah chapter 3. In his anger, he prayed that God would kill him. When we receive our calling, we need to identify our emotional state before taking action. We always want to be ready for the worst about the unknown. The doctor in my stroke case said they had to do the same in telling the family the worst case scenario while hoping for the best. Why would a good God put you in a bad situation? Because favor is operable by God in His choice to show man that they cannot control every situation.

God used his anger to beautifully illustrate His point to show us how He uses favor by the way He used Jonah's dilemma to demonstrate the power of His favor. For example, God used a little plant and a worm to show that Jonah had no right to get to this level of anger in his life. After allowing a little plant to grow in one day, he sent a worm to attack the plant which caused it to dry up and die (Jonah 4:7). Needless to say, Jonah got the point. In today's modern world, there are distractions before us all. We must get the point immediately to avoid missed opportunities to share Jesus with a hurt and dying world.

Another instance where people get lost compares to Jonah's time in the belly of the fish. Many have started to view this story as a fairy tale, so they miss the entire sequence. The reason any of you are reading this book is because you are or have been in the belly of a fish. That means you have made some decisions that have landed you in tight, isolated spots. But there is good news: God had the fish spit Jonah out right where he was supposed to, at the right time to get Jonah to agree to do what God had commanded him.

There was nothing Jonah tried to do that would work. The same story is true for many people outside the will of God. For you to say yes, is a joy to be found in the Master's good pleasure. It is understandable how His goodness would follow you all the days of your life when you are in His favor.

This is a very common experience for people handling a call. We see the Jonah phenomenon when something bad happens to us at the wrong time, such as losing our job. It was the sun that forced Jonah to echo his previous sentiment of wanting to just die as a means of escaping his dilemma. At the presence of the hot sun from the east, Jonah felt a sense of helplessness and requested once again that God would just kill him. This is news for anyone who has been called: God is not going to kill you at your request. Just as no man knows when the end is coming, we cannot have a shortcut by requesting death. God is not the author of death, but life.

Knowing what we are deciding and how we are living must be a priority because we are ever in the presence of the almighty God. It is not time to continue being impressed about the accomplishments of this life, but rather to know that God adds treasures that are stored up pending your rest in Him. That must be a resounding message to the called of God. He wants to use you, but if you are not willing, He does have others that He has called also.

In accepting the call of God, it was mentioned earlier in this book that it is God's goal and

mission to reach those who have not received His message yet. According to scriptures, during Jonah's day, He mentioned that there were 120,000 souls in Nineveh that had not been reached. In Jonah's case, what we see here is wasted time. When we put off the call of God, when looking behind us, it is often considered wasted time outside of relevant ministry. He's going to accomplish His will through you no matter what. So it has to be our will to please Him in every way of our life. Recalling Jonah's story is a reminder of how God has preordained plans and shows that man cannot go wrong in obedience to God, and by following His agenda versus our own.

That was pretty much my story during my youth. I remember when I scored my first job as a teen, my father reminded me not forget to tithe. I replied, "God and I have an understanding." I can honestly say that I was not ready for the call of God, but only for the world and its variety of sins. Now mature, I see the importance of serving Him in an understanding way and operating in obedience. It's important to go where He tells us to go, when He says go.

Chapter 5 Review

A Time of Reflection

1. In your imagination, what did Jonah picture a calling's rate of return to be?

2. How does the captain on the ship relate to people in your life?

3. What was the purpose of the little plant and the worm?

4. Describe "wasted time" in executing relevant ministry.

5. What is classified as His plans versus our agenda?

Chapter 6

THE ULTIMATE CALL: THE CALL OF JEREMIAH

Prophecy and speaking in unknown languages will become useless. But love will last forever. (1 Corinthians 13:8, NLT)

Love is often misunderstood and miscommunicated due to the various ways it can be expressed. In the Greek language alone, there are many ways it can be exhibited. For example, the first form of love that is demonstrated without fail is by God. Psalm 21:7 shares that "the king trusts in The Lord and His (the Lord) love is unfailing and it will keep you from stumbling." Knowing that God's love is dependable should give us all the assurance we need to accomplish what He has designed for His will through our lives such as the calling.

The word agape means unconditional love. The word eros connotes an erotic, sexual or emotional love, such as with your wife or husband. The third type, storg, signifies the type of love a family shares. The final word we will look at is philia, is a mental love as shown in our brotherly love relationships.

We primarily receive agape love when accepting the call. Whether or not you agree to do so, calls for God to live in the agape because the price was already paid to show how He loves us by the giving of His only son, Jesus, on the cross. God demonstrates His love in this: that He would give His Son in the death on a cross because He loved us while we were still sinners. (Romans 5:8)

The next calling we want to discuss involves a young man named Jeremiah. In a one-on-one moment with God, Jeremiah was told by God that He knew him before he was in his mother's womb, that he had been chosen.

Jeremiah's work was ordained by God. He chose to send Jeremiah to the world as a prophet unto the nations. Ironically, we've only seen the calling of prophets in Moses, Samuel, Jonah and now Jeremiah. Due to dispensation, many schools of thought do not believe God still calls apostles and prophets. But due to the effectiveness of the modern church, we have to believe that He does. (Ephesians 4:11-13)

According to Hebrews 13:7, Jesus Christ is the same yesterday, today, and forevermore. So if He equipped the church for the work of service during biblical days, isn't He still providing today? Of course He is. Despite differing theological stances, He is the living

God who resurrected Christ from the dead by His miraculous power. He uses apostles to establish a strong foundation for new and existing churches. Prophets are used to deliver tough messages to correct words and warn against sin in the church. Evangelists are used by God to proclaim the gospel to those who have not heard it. Pastors are the caretakers of the flock, which is their congregation. Finally, teachers in a church are responsible for distributing the gospel and the Word for Bible based instruction. Clearly, it is possible for God to call apostles and prophets through the offices in the church.

Jeremiah responded just as many of us would: with an excuse. He used his age as an excuse. He said that he was too young and that his speech was not sophisticated enough. Is there anything that is young in God's eyesight? Is anyone too young to be called by God for His calling, marriage, the military, or occupation.

Our age is based on perspectives in our culture of minimum age requirements. We see in Jeremiah that there are no age requirements with God. He was told to go wherever God sent him and say whatever God told him. This word is still the command today for the called of God. It requires a denial of our self wants and needs.

We must take on the mindset of being in the military. We are, in fact, in the Lord's army. Men and women in the military can't simply go where they want to or do whatever they please. They have to take and follow commands. What was great about Jeremiah's instructions was that God immediately told him to say what he tells him, and God would protect him from there. Afterwards, he touched Jeremiah's mouth to give him this command. This is assurance for the called. His words are accurate, precise and true. We are told in scripture that the truth shall set you free. (John 8:32)

Unlike many unbelievers, there is a lot of freedom exercised in believers to reign in their lives. In 1 Corinthians 3:20, it states "that wherever the spirit of The Lord is there is freedom." Many times, the call is not accepted because believers are not ready to let something go. The refusal to release a stronghold in our lives is having the freedom to sin.

Authority is an essential dynamic exercised in the Christian ministry. Authority does not mean showing overconfidence in oneself. It is not cockiness or any earthly characteristic, but rather it is a unique display of humility and God's unmatched power. Authority is the tool that Jesus places within all Christians through the Holy Spirit. If you feel that you are lacking authority in the Spirit, stop reading and pray for a positive spiritual esteem and recollection of all the times He has never left or forsaken you.

Chapter 6 Review

A TIME OF REFLECTION

1. Please name the various types of love and their meanings.

2. Does it help or hurt to know what you are called to even if you do not like it?

3. What are you battling with releasing so that you can fulfill your calling?

4. What are the five offices of the church?

5. What is the assurance for the called?

Chapter 7

THE IMPORTANCE OF MENTORSHIP IN YOUR CALLING: THE CALLING OF ELISHA

Onesimus has not been of use to you in the past, but now he is of use to you and me. (Philemon 1:11, NKJV)

So Elijah went over to him and threw his cloak across his shoulders and then walked away (1 Kings 19:19). The cloak was his mantle which embodied power and superiority in his office. Due to Elijah's fear in dealing with Jezebel, God was making a decision to replace him with an even greater man with a subservient spirit. Elisha was looking forward to finishing business as he destroyed his plow, showing there will not be a change of mind to return to the plow.

Elijah and Elisha were a perfect tandem for the passing of the mantle because of their obedient spirits. One obeyed from the standpoint of releasing his role, while the other one accepted his role, though Elisha still submitted to Elijah's authority.

In your calling, know that you may have to face this scenario in the local church. Always maintain a good attitude when you work for The Lord. Remind yourself that it all belongs to Him (Psalms 24:1). This is the key to having and being a mentor. There must be someone you can bounce things that you do not understand off of.

This, by far, is the most interesting look at the call. Elisha was busy at work plowing with his oxen when Elijah passed by and put his mantle on him (1 Kings 19:19). He was working in his secular vocation. How many are in that place? When I was in corporate America, it was difficult trying to balance my love for the Word of God, moving up the corporate ladder, maintaining integrity to do an ethical thing by the company, and taking care of personal responsibilities.

What was interesting about Elisha was that his response to the call was to destroy his oxen. We must be cognizant of our allegiance to our secular commitments when weighing our decisions regarding the call of God. He pledged his oxen as a sacrifice when he was fully committed. When Elijah passed by him and threw his robe over him, Elisha's running after him signifies Elisha's hunger and thirst to be a man of God, with Elijah as his role model. Please make sure you identify a mentor when you accept your calling.

The Importance of Mentorship in your Calling: The Calling of Elisha

A key element to know when making a decision about your calling is identity. You must know who you are, and as the past generation said, "Know whose you are!" Ephesians 1:3 shares "that we are blessed with every spiritual blessing in the heavenlies." The word blessed in this scripture is eulogia. Eulogia is where we get our English word for eulogy. It means "He has spoken well over us." God has plans stored in advance for the provision of human beings. Think about the last time you went to a funeral. They never said a negative word about the deceased, even though they may have lived their life away from God's standard. He has planned for us even before the world was created (Ephesians 2:10). If He speaks well about us, then why shouldn't we speak well of ourselves. On the other hand, one of the most difficult things to address when experiencing the call is personal relationships. It is wise to ask a girl or guy while dating, "Would you marry me if I had to preach the gospel?"

Elisha asked Elijah if he could kiss his mother and father goodbye. It was upon going back that Elisha made a sacrifice, said goodbye, and fed some people that were there. His ministry had already begun. He was found with a servant's heart at the onset of his ministry. Please take a moment in prayer and reflect upon the condition of your heart. Upon accepting your calling, you must be humble enough to do whatever it takes as a condition of your calling. As Elisha cooked and distributed the food, the scriptures say that he became Elijah's assistant.

Being an assistant in ministry may mean many things. Remember that there are five offices in the church that require assistance: prophets, apostles, evangelists, pastors, and teachers. It is important to know this because there is a movement in churches that allow people to assist leaders of the church under the name of being an armor bearer.

An armor bearer is an Old Testament terminology that ended in the New Covenant. It was used to signify a dedicated servant of The Lord. This is what many ministries are doing to display servitude in the name of the Lord. I am not saying that no one should become an armor bearer, but this is merely a warning to understand why are you doing it. What is your motive?

Elisha's leader, Elijah, was with the King of Samaria's messenger when he questioned them about their belief in God before prophesying their death. An assistant should seek directions and follow an example of ministry before going along independently.

Ministers are going independent through pride, leading to the huge number of church plant failures in the United States. Everyone should have a mentor. Christ instructs us to go make disciples. So why is there not a strong commitment by Christians to make disciples? Many may fear being a disciple for a lack of knowledge (Hosea 4:6). The more likely reason is they are preoccupied with life and have used their distractions to be pulled away from God.

Chapter 7 Review

A TIME OF REFLECTION

1. What represents your power "mantle" today?

2. Identify a key characteristic that you must possess and Elisha had?

3. Where have you been found at work?

4. What are you willing to sacrifice for the calling?

5. What ministry direction have you been following?

Chapter 8

EVENTS FROM THE VISION

God blesses the one who reads the words of this prophecy to the church and he blesses all who listen to its message and obey what it says. (Revelation 1:3, NKJV)

When I was in my coma, the Lord had shown me that I had executed my call effectively and was walking in it, but there was going to be more. Jeremiah 33:3 says, call to Me and I will answer you and show you things you know nothing about (NKJV). This revealed to me that God is still the God of mysteries. I understood the depth of God, that He has the ability to be omnipresence: existing in a far place but able to be near at the same time. While I was in a comatose state, this became an aspect of God's depth that I grew to understand firsthand on a more experiential basis. We must realize that the deep calls out to deep (Psalm 42:7). I had a relationship with Him, but the next level of my calling required a break from business or ministry as usual, and a deeper spiritual intimacy.

On my first night of my vision while in the coma, I saw myself sickened and flown out to Glendale, California. While in Glendale, I was whisked to a surgery center that was at the building where I previously worked while in living in Southern California. While there, I saw Jesus conferring with two surgeons at the surgical board, though there was not surgery performed on this or any other trip. After I finished watching Jesus talking with the surgeons, it was then that I discovered that I could still walk. Once they were finished with the evaluation, I discovered then that I could no longer walk. I was back home with no surgical procedure or anything. I never had a pearly gate experience; I simply heard the words "I'm not ready for you yet, because I already got you."

It was very assuring to hear that message in the midst of my trial. From there, the vision continued for the next five days of my coma, and now I saw myself back home in Houston, Texas. While back at home, I saw that I became sick again. It is very strange that my illness was occurring in the natural but not in the spirit. Next, I was referred to a privatized location in northwest Houston, Texas. They delivered me to a surgical center approximately twenty minutes from our home. After studying the locale of the facility, I found out that it was located in a residential neighborhood that I use to live in.

Events From the Vision

After coming out of anesthesia, my attendees in the surgical suite were nurses that were angels. The angels in these visions were former members affiliated with my church, or people involved in the missions field. They were presented in their unmarried states. They took very gentle care, promoting a family attitude. During recovery, they escorted my wife, three kids, and mother into the surgery room. That's when I realized I was sick in the natural, but I could not break out of the coma at this realization.

As my ailment continued, I saw in the vision that now I had been flown to Indianapolis, Indiana. At this location, I recognized that there were not any personnel present except nurses, and the Chief Surgeon was Jesus Christ. It was here that my family was also escorted in to be with me during this surgical procedure. So as you can see, family plays a big role in my life and ministry. While in Indiana, I had some visions within the vision.

It was while I was in Indiana, where I have never visited, that I found myself in a surgical suite in Brazil, before immediately being found in Raymondville, Texas. In this vision in Brazil, I knew that my wife and kids were in the surgical suite with me. In the natural, the report was that I probably wouldn't make it through the night. Another report on the second day was that I would not be the same but I would live and be a vegetable.

In Indianapolis, I had a vision within the vision placing me in Brazil where I saw God shining a big light over a cornfield. After doing this over some children for a while, He got bored and said to me, "Now you shine it." This part of the vision really threw me for a loop, as we were already working and being faithful in both real life and ministry (2 Timothy 2:2).

After accepting His command, I was then shown in San Andreas, Columbia. It was weird being here because they were searching everywhere for a place to do surgery. I then saw Jesus turn to my mother and say, "If there is nothing wrong with his heart, we don't need to operate on it." Then the vision shifted to Guatemala and Yugoslavia.

The whole vision is still a mystery, as it very well could be a reflection of my life. I have traveled and ministered in half of the cities we visited during the vision. I have not ministered or been to the countries of Brazil, Yugoslavia, Guatemala, or to the city of Indianapolis. Coincidentally, my wife was just returning from Guatemala on John Maxwell Public Speaking business a week before I had my stroke.

What all of this means is still a mystery, so in the meantime I'll focus on identifying my calling in detail and how it has changed and expanded. The Lord had my wife and I resign from our leadership in church ministry to place more emphasis on our business dealing with marriages so that we can reach more couples outside the church.

In addition, there has been a calling to meet the needs of the disabled (particularly those that have brain injuries). I really don't know what God has planned. But do I ever? "The faith walk is ever so rewarding" (Hebrews 11:6), "for we walk by faith and not by sight" (2 Corinthians 5:7).

Many of my family have experienced dreams of me walking across stages and performing household duties like mowing the yard, doing dishes, and vacuuming. They even saw me running. This is good news given that I have small kids. Having kids and a great wife have also aided in my healing process.

My friend, Arthur, and his son, Isaiah, were instrumental in helping me to walk in my personal time. They committed to come over to my house two times a week, and we walked in my neighborhood faithfully. Whiling walking, we discussed the scriptures that gave me extra insight into the necessity of fellowship and the body of Christ. Through their presence, I was able to experience the love of Christ. They fulfilled one of the chief emotional needs of a brain recovering patient: social fulfillment. Social fulfillment is key for the believer, but do not let it occupy your time or dominate your schedule. Identify two people that you are in fellowship with weekly, so that you can begin to interact with them in a healthy relationship.

Chapter 8 Review

A TIME OF REFLECTION

1. Discuss what does "deep calls unto deep: mean in Psalms 42:7?

2. Immediately, what was racing through your mind as you read about the visions?

3. Do you believe in visions, church offices, callings, and strange things of God?

Chapter 9

PERSONAL TIME MINISTRY

For the person who has entered His rest has rested from his works, as God did from His. (Hebrews 4:10, HCSB)

When a person can't walk, they must enter rehabilitation. When I finally woke up from my coma, after being transferred to a second hospital that specialized in helping people in their next stage of recovery, I discovered that I could not walk in reality. So I was enrolled in a program consisting of physical therapy to address my walking, occupational therapy to address the motion of my limbs and to help out with the tasks of daily life, and speech therapy to assist me with talking again since the stroke, as well as the insertion of a tracheotomy on four different occasions, damaged my ability to speak. The only therapies I was not enrolled in were music and water therapy.

When I first matriculated into rehabilitation after my stroke, I could not stand, walk, get dressed, tie my shoes, talk, or eat properly. After four months, I was able to master all. What happens when the therapists fail to incorporate the right plan? It definitely delays the process. Based on the severity of patients' injuries, there are no two care plans that should be exactly the same. A stroke victim should be treated differently than a spinal cord patient. The bottom line is to still have the same results, but the approach is different in how it is accomplished.

The same is applicable in spiritual rehabilitation. Every person on this earth must be prescribed a spiritual rehabilitation program so God can receive His glory from their life. When rehabilitation is effective, one must tell others of how they achieved such great outcomes. The same principle applies in our spiritual lives.

The commitment to therapy reminds me of our spiritual life. I was unfamiliar with therapy, but it led me to focus on God. This focus on the total healing process was unbelievable, even by the doctor's standard, who had declared I would not make it through the night or that I would be a vegetable. Clearly I have the prevailing, redeeming power of Jesus Christ. He had already paid the blood price for my sins and healing. The human body is designed to heal itself based on the stripes rendered to Christ. The Texas Medical Center statistics say that two out of every seven patients survive from my type of stroke, but are not able to have a very productive life. I am one of those two, and I seek to do the impossible. For, by God, all things are possible. This is the mindset you must have when beginning a spiritual or physical rehabilitation program.

A spiritual rehabilitation program is relevant to a person who has been away from the Lord for years or has never known Him. The spiritual and physical rehabilitation requires a heart transformation. Help will be needed. Just as there are therapists present to assist the patient in walking, speaking, and functioning, there also needs to be spiritual therapists present in our society to ease people through their past church hurts, family crises, and life's disappointments.

As a Christian, we all have spiritual therapists. Jesus commanded us to go into the world and make disciples, baptizing them in the name of the Father, Son, and the Holy Spirit (Matthew 28:20). As we do this, He promises to be with us to the end of time. The assurance of the end of time is the way any rehabilitation should be approached.

Chapter 9 Review

A Time of Reflection

1. How should Christians be enrolled in a spiritual rehabilitation program?

2. What percentage of patients have hemorrhage strokes?

3. In your opinion, in regards to such a serious injury such as a stroke, what was its purpose related to the calling?

Chapter 10

WHERE FROM HERE

And I am certain of this, that He that began a good work in you, will continue his work until it is finished on the day when Christ Jesus returns. (Philippians 1:6)

When considering blessings, everyday I'm reminded of Isaiah 54:17 which states, "No weapon formed against me shall prosper, and every tongue that rises against me in judgment shall be condemned, this is the heritage of the servants of The Lord." This passage, as well as all scripture, echoes as true. It validates all the claims that we've made in regards to me surviving from a rare type of stroke and perceiving as a stroke of Favor from God.

During my stroke episode, my friend and boss, Mike Barber, told me that the last thing I said in consciousness was, "Devil, get away from me." That is why I believe I'm still alive to tell of His goodness.

Prior to that, he said that I quoted "I am healed in Jesus' name," as I realized something was going majorly wrong heath-wise.

This was a great self-testimony that exemplified that during adversity the Word and disciplines of the Spirit are valuable to accomplish overcoming the weapons of the world and the enemy. By using faith during a crisis, we place the action of God on call. Allow me to remind you that He is a rewarder of faith. That reward might be the saving of a life, as it was in my case, or getting a job, interceding for someone else, or whatever request you may desire.

In relation, there is a man I read about on Yahoo named Ted Bartling. Ted was a rocket scientist by trade. One Day, he made a decision to donate his kidney to a young toddler. He was hailed as a hero by the media and general public. Psalm 16:3 in the NIV declares that the godly shall be my hero. That is a great classification system in determining a hero.

In our lives as adults, we've grown to not believe in heroes. Many people are the same in their faith systems. We believed strongly in heroes as kids. We believed that despite their human appearance that they were able to fly, freeze things, pick up buildings, and cars, etc. In the faith, we must maintain this super belief. According to Mark 10:15, it is said that disciples should have child-like faith to inherit the kingdom of heaven.

Jesus said our faith needs to be the size of a mustard seed. Imagine that such a big figure as God mentioning something as small as a mustard seed. The mustard seed is so small that one can barely pinch it, but it yields a large harvest. In this life, our judgment of rewards will be on the type of harvest that was produced, and how we did stewarding the harvest we were involved in. In Ted's case, this was a lot of the consideration in his decision. He considered another more important than Himself. This is the example of how favor overflows in our life through serving and humility as we emulate the life of Jesus Christ. In doing so, this favor comes in handy for favors of suffering where God uses them to rescue the righteous suffering in the midst of affliction. In this state, God will turn what's meant for bad into what's good.

Chapter 10 Review

A TIME OF REFLECTION

1. What work in specific are you trusting God to complete in your life?

2. How has adversity shaped your ministry?

3. The Bible declares in Psalms 16:3 that the godly shall be my hero. By reflecting on Ted Bartling's heroisms, how would you view the Christian's role in this function?

4. God's favor is available to all believers. How has He placed favor in your life?

5. Discuss and reflect upon holiness. In what ways must you improve in some area to satisfy God's plan for you.

Chapter 11

GOD'S FAVOR IN THE CALL

When we are faithless, our God remains faithful. He cannot deny Himself. (2 Timothy 2:13, HSBC)

As a parent of three girls, it would be unfair if I showed favoritism of one over another. It's the same way with God, as He is a just and a good God (Psalms 111:7). He loves all believers the same way. "For God so loved the world that He gave His begotten Son that whoever believes should not perish but have eternal life (John 3:16), and the Bible declares that God demonstrated His love in this that while we were sinners Christ died for us (Romans 5:8). He paid forward a most powerful price because, although He knew of us before the world was formed, we had not been manifested in the flesh at the time of His decision to favor mankind and to defeat a spiritual enemy forever through one kind gesture given for millions.

One thing the Lord may do is allow an employer to offer you a raise. At another point another person gets one, but you don't. The way that the other person that is not getting a raise behaves when you do determines at what times and the types of blessings are granted unto a person. This a condition of the heart. God is the sole determinate of this condition. For person one, their blessing of favor may primarily occur at the workplace, while person two is experiencing them in their personal life. This is because God chooses when to distribute earthly favor in a person's life.

In the calling, favor is shown in a plurality of ways. That is why it is key to have a personal relationship with God. This is the first step. The way to activate God's favor is by following the advice of David, who has been labeled as the apple of God's eye (where it is written "Let the words of my mouth and the meditation of my heart be acceptable in your sight" (Psalm 19:14, NSJV). God communicates through the spirit of a heart. God is a spirit and those that worship Him, worship Him in spirit and truth (John 4:24).

Favor is a byproduct of grace. Since grace is known in our culture as undeserved merit. How about defining it as undeserved favor. An example would be when you were apart from God living a life of sin, and He allowed you to live to accept Christ twenty years after you left home and became saved. It was favor exacted on your life that allowed for Him to save you at the moment you chose Jesus as your Lord and Savior.

The many ways God delivers His favor on your life in the call are things such as helping you meet financial obligations, healing you or family or fellow church member during illness, bringing to your remembrance by the Holy Spirit a word during a message that was not thoroughly prepared correctly, a gift, education, and many other things. Remember the earth is His and everything in it. So, it is easy for God to grant you earthly things. Some things we must pray for specifically, but other things He gives us because He loves us beyond our human comprehension or understanding. The way that we view ourselves when analyzing His calling over our lives is always inaccurate. Yes, it should be mind boggling, but He grows us into being able to perform the aspects of the call that He requires. This view should be taken because we must be constantly mindful that our God is holy so therefore, we must be holy (1 Peter 1:16).

The believer that handles the call of God must be pursuing Him in holiness. Holiness is a spiritual discipline in and of itself. In today's modern world, one may ask, "How am I supposed to exercise holiness with all distractions away from God in my life?" That's precisely the point. When one lives a holy life, it is their aim to try to be just like God. This is confirmed in the book of Matthew as a reminder for us to "Be holy for your Father in heaven is holy" (Matthew 5:48).

Often times, believers that walk in holiness are treated as if they are weird and are definitely misunderstood. This is why the writings of the Apostle Peter show the early church Christians were referred to as aliens. An alien is an extraterrestrial being that does not belong to this world. Furthermore, in 1 John 2:15, Christ also defined the Christian's status by instructing believers, "Do not love the world or the things that belong to the world," Loving the things of this world is where many believers are thrown off track in the desire to live holy. In life, it is either one thing or the other. Christ said that man could not love God and mammon (Matthew 6:24). The decision to choose between the seen and the unseen is often the choice that inheritors of eternal life have to make. We must always be mindful, in our walks and calling, that our citizenship is in heaven and we eagerly await our Savior, The Lord Jesus Christ. (Philippians 3:20).

Having to choose between God and mammon, or money, can be correlated to hearing the call of God and choosing to ignore it and press on your career pursuits. This may exist for a couple of reasons:

1) Fear–God has stated in 2 Timothy 1:7 that He has not given believers a spirit of fear but of love, power, and a sound mine. If we allow fear to cause us to miss God's will for our lives by making the decision to avoid the calling, it has a deeper impact outside of our lives here on earth, for it involves eternity and the accountability of not going to others that you were supposed to take the word to.

2) The love of money–In the scriptures, 1 Timothy 6:10 states that the love of money is the root for all kinds of evil things, and because of it many have wandered away from the faith. When denying God's call for this reason, you realize that the last state of the believer is worse off than the first. You go from being a faithful saint to being a disobedient, missing leader.

These are the two most common and pertinent reasons for avoiding the call of God. He has equipped you with everything that you need to be obedient and successful. Maybe you are already successful in the corporate business world. Be confident that God has blessed you there. He'll bless you as an ambassador of Christ that was created to do work in Him before the foundation of the world was established.

We must understand that when one receives the call of God, they have his favor. This type of favor surpasses human understanding of favor. As humans, we often receive favor as preferential treatment, but with God there is no selection process. The scriptures declare that God is no respecter of persons (Acts 10:34, HSBC). This is because He loves all His children equally. We all have the right to accept the gospel. We all are given free will to live with or to without Him. We are all extended grace unto us, and have all received His favor in different ways.

By receiving favor, it is like another calling that many are already involved in: marriage. God states in the Bible, "When a man takes a wife, He finds a good thing and obtains favor from The Lord" (Proverbs 18:22). Marriage is a sacred, holy institution created by God here on earth with Adam and Eve. As such, we must follow the same intimate details of our individual walks with Him. Always remain joyful, you are married to the Father, therefore His favor rests upon you.

Chapter 11 Review

A TIME OF REFLECTION

1. When you experienced your calling, what major event was occurring or getting ready to happen in your life at that time?

2. What happened in your earlier or previous relationship with God?

3. What qualifies you to serve the audience that you feel called to?

4. Write an outline about what you feel called to. (Hosea 2:2) How do you know?

5. Who have you shared aspects of your calling with? Who is counseling you? Who is leading you along?

6. What will happen spiritually, emotionally and physically if you do not pursue this call?

7. How much time, attention, and research are you applying daily to understanding your calling?

8. Are you keeping a journal of both your calling and your relationship with Christ? Are you failing to share information in this journal about your calling? If Yes, what is it?

Contact information for bookings:

Michael and Danielle Ward

truelove@ilovemarriage.com

www.ingramcontent.com/pod-product-compliance
Ingram Content Group UK Ltd.
Pitfield, Milton Keynes, MK11 3LW, UK
UKHW041955230426
12048UKWH00008B/362